This book
belongs to:

. . . .

. . . .

How to use this book:

Alphablocks helps children learn to read, from their first encounter with letters and sounds to independent reading. It is all about engaging children's interest and having fun with words. *D's Drumming Din* introduces children to four new letters and sounds, as taught in Reception and in some Nursery classes: **I**, **N**, **M** and **D**. This book is designed for an adult and child to enjoy together. Here are some tips:

• Call the Alphablocks by their letter sounds, not by their letter names - this helps your child learn the letter sounds.

• Try to say a short **mmm**, not 'muh', and so on, for the consonant letter sounds. The vowel sound **i** is the starting sound of 'ink'.

• Try running your finger along the words as you read: this gives your child the idea of how reading works. After a few reads, encourage your child to read the letter sounds to you.

• The magic words the Alphablocks make are for your child to read. Tap each Alphablock and say its sound, then blend the sounds to read the whole word.

Reading should be a fun experience and never a chore. Be sure to catch your child in the right mood and let them tell you when they've had enough. You can use the activities at the back of the book as a reward for great reading!

You can find out more about Alphablocks and reading at **www.alphablocks.tv**

First published in Great Britain in 2015 by Egmont UK Limited,
The Yellow Building, 1 Nicholas Road, London W11 4AN

Original illustrations © Alphablocks Ltd 2010-2015
Alphablocks logo © Alphablocks Ltd 2010

ISBN 978 1 4052 7835 5
59911/1
Printed in Italy

Alphablocks

D's Drumming Din

There's a sound in Alphaland – **d**! **d**! **d**! It's **D**. **D** loves loud drumming but he has no drums. It's a disaster!

Here comes **A**. "**a**! **a**! **a**!" she says as apples drop on her head.

Can you make a **d**! **d**! **d**! sound, like **D**? It's the sound **D** makes when he **drums**.

"**p**! **p**! **p**!" says **P**, popping in.
Perhaps **P** and **A** can help **D** ...

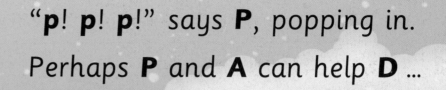

Help **P**, **A** and **D** do **word magic**.

p a d

p-a-d, pad!

A pad of paper! **D** is disappointed.
"I definitely can't drum with that!"
he despairs. Perhaps **N** will help.

"**n**! **n**! **n**! No! Not now! Never!" says **N**. But then **N** remembers how much he likes noise and joins in after all!

Can you make a **n**! **n**! **n**! sound, like **N**? It's the sound **N** makes when he means **no**.

Help **P**, **A** and **N** do **word magic**.

p a n

p-a-n, pan!

A pan! Now **D** is doubly disappointed.
"Not good for noise," says **N**. "Noise is
nice, we must try again."

So this time **I** comes
to help. "**i! i! i!**" sings
I importantly.

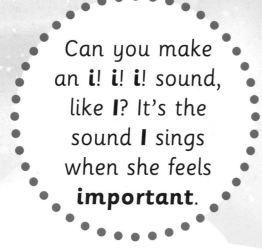

Can you make an **i**! **i**! **i**! sound, like **I**? It's the sound **I** sings when she feels **important**.

Help **P**, **I** and **N** do **word magic**.

p-i-n, pin!

"A pin and a pad and a pan are pathetic," says **P**. **D** is downhearted. He has lots of Alphablocks friends ready to play in his band but no instruments.

"**t**! **t**! **t**! Time to try something different," says **T**.

Help **T**, **A** and **P** do **word magic**.

t a p

t-a-p, tap!

Everyone taps their toes. **T** taps the pan.
A taps the pad and **P** taps the pin.

"Nice noise,"
nods **N**.
"Definitely,"
decides **D**.

"m! m! m!" agrees **M**, "but more band mates would make more music."

Can you make a **m**! **m**! **m**! sound, like **M**? It's the sound **M** makes when he **munches**.

Help **M**, **A** and **N** do **word magic**.

m-a-n, man!

A man! A singing gingerbread man. "Run, run as fast as you can!" he sings.

"No," shouts **N**.
"No running. Let's
make noise instead!"

"**i**! **i**! **i**! I think I can help," says **I**.

Help **D**, **I** and **N** do **word magic**.

d-i-n, din! At last **D** has drums!

"Let's do it," shouts **D** as he bangs on the drums. What a din!

"This is nice and noisy," says **N**, and everyone joins in with **D**'s din, dancing until they are dizzy!

The End

Can you make a din, with all these new sounds? **d**! **d**! **d**! **i**! **i**! **i**! **m**! **m**! **m**! **n**! **n**! **n**! – nice!

Now turn over to practise everything you've learnt today.

Mmm, marvellous!

M loves to munch marvellous meals.
Point to the tasty pictures on this page that begin with the **m** sound.

Make **m** ! **m** ! **m** ! sounds each time you see some food or drink beginning with the **m** sound.

Do the action

Rub your tummy and pretend to hold some food you want to munch, saying **m! m! m!**

What a din!

It's not just **D** who makes a din. Some of these animals are noisy too. Use your finger to trace a **d** at the start of each animal's name.

d

dragon

deer

donkey

duck

dog

Do the action
Pretend to play the drums, saying **d! d! d!**

Night napping!

Look at these two pictures of **N** and his friends at night. They're not the same. 5 things are not right in the second picture. Shout "no!" each time you notice one. Night-night **N**. Nap time!

Do the action
Fold your arms and shake your head for 'no', saying **n**! **n**! **n**!

I and M in a muddle

Follow the muddled lines to match **I** to the words beginning with the **i** sound and **M** to the words beginning with the **m** sound! Say the **i** and **m** sounds as you follow the lines.

i

m

Do the action
Hold out your arms to show how important you are and sing **i! i! i!**

ink

You can read!

Look at all the words you can read now!

Make word magic with each of these words and then find the pictures that match.

m - a - n

p - a - d

m - a - p

m - a - t

p - i - n

I, N, M and **D** say goodbye.
Now you've met them, they'll be
your reading friends for life!

i n m d